Contents

Contents ....
Introduction ....
Recipes
    Carrot, green olive, cilantro (coriander) ....
    Cucumber, walnut, orange ....
    Potato, spring onion, ham ....
    Zucchini (courgette), radish, date 1
    Cannellini beans, pear 1
    Fig, radicchio, endive (chicory) 1
    Chinese cabbage, bamboo shoots 1
    Carrot, radish, nuts 1
    Tomato, goat cheese, olive 2
    Green salad 2
    Tomato, pureed corn 2
    Curried egg mayonnaise ....
    Tomato and cucumber gelatin ....
    Carrot, pine nut, parsley 3
    Tofu, shallot, raison 3
    Rice, cilantro (coriander), strawberry 3
    Beetroot, yoghurt, chive, red onion, parsley 3
    Fennel, goat cheese, grape 3
    Celery, radish, dried apricot 4
    Red cabbage, pepper, tomato 4
    Lentil, zucchini (courgette), spinach 4
    Banana, nut, fig 4
    Carrot, zucchini (courgette), chive 4
    Brussels sprout, mushroom 5
    Pinto, green bean, beetroot 5
    Spinach, fennel, walnut 5
    Corn, tomato, leek 5
    Brown rice, carrot, cress ....
    Winter salad 6
    Tomato, tofu, spring onion 6
    Celery, grape, nut 6
    Cauliflower, radish, zucchini (courgette) 6
    Bean, onion, cheese 6
    Nut and raison ball 7
    Root vegetables 7
    Sprout, kiwi, avocado 7
    Carrot, chilly, olive, nut 7
    Endive (chicory), grapefruit, date 7

© 2018, Victor Saumarez. All rights reserved. No part of this book may be reproduced or transmitted in any form any means, electronic, mechanical, photocopying, recording, or otherwise, without the prior written permission the publisher. **Notice of Liability.** *The information in this book is distributed on an "as-is" basis, without warrant While every precaution is taken in the preparation of the book, the author and publisher shall not have any liabili to any person or entity either in respect to any losses or damage caused or alleged to be caused directly or indirect by instructions contained in this book or by food choices and preparation described in it.*

Introduction

This book is dedicated to my late mother, Julia, who inspired many of the ideas behind the recipes that follow. She was the founder, director and driving force behind Shrubland Hall Health Clinic, a leading establishment of its kind in Europe. It was so ahead of its time some of its guiding principles concerning health are only now coming into vogue. I served my salad-making apprenticeship under her watchful eye. I was also a salad chef for Cranks, one of London's foremost vegetarian restaurants.

The purpose of the book is to inspire those wishing to lead a healthier lifestyle with ways of creating tasty and wholesome meals from mostly fresh, raw vegetables. There is no secret formula to creating salads. You can combine almost any vegetable with any other for a pleasing and nourishing meal or side dish. The possibilities for combining colors, textures, and tastes are endless. The recipes that follow offer several ideas of what is possible.

The health benefits of eating vegetables and fruit are considerable and include the lowering of blood pressure, reducing the risk of heart disease, and may even help in the prevention of certain cancers. Leafy green vegetables are thought to be particularly effective in combatting cardiovascular disease and reducing blood pressure. Tomatoes in particular contain properties that help reduce the risk of prostate cancer in men. Stomach acidity, bowel movement, energy levels, and sleep can all be improved with a healthy diet.

Meal preparation often takes a back seat in our modern hectic lives. Food has been relegated to its basic function; that of merely providing fuel for the energy we need to cope with our daily challenges. Convenience dictates what, when and how we eat. This gives rise to poor eating habits that can lead, in some cases, to severe ill health. It's no coincidence that in cultures where food preparation is taken seriously there is a lower rate of food-related illnesses leading to greater longevity. By introducing salads into our daily eating routines, food-related health risks begin to fall away.

As with any form of cooking, salad preparation can be a rewarding experience on so many levels. Salads are quick and easy to prepare leaving minimal mess to clean up afterwards. While embracing the challenges of modern day living they also ensure we get the essential ingredients needed to function optimally. It is an art form.

There is no sincerer love than the love of food.
George Bernard Shaw

Carrot, Green Olive, and Cilantro

This works well as a starter, or as an accompaniment to chicken or fish. The aromatic flavor of the coriander and nutty sesame oil give this recipe an unusual and subtle taste, while the olive gives it a little more bite.

Ingredients

Carrot
Green olive
Cilantro (coriander)
Sesame oil
Lemon juice
Black pepper
Sea salt

Preparation

Coarsely grate the carrot. If you leave carrot to stand for any length of time, add a little lemon juice to prevent discoloration. Leave olives whole, or chop into slices, remove large stalks from the coriander, toss together until the texture is a pleasing mix.

Dressing

Sesame oil and lemon juice work well with this salad. Add some black pepper, and a pinch of salt to taste.

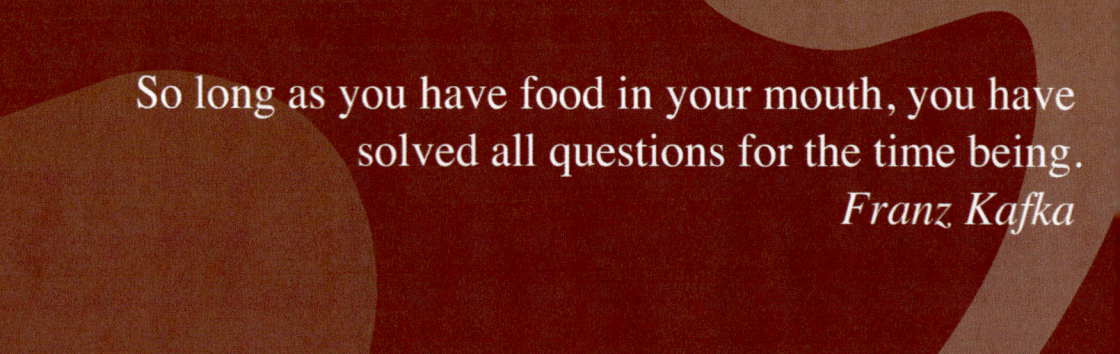

So long as you have food in your mouth, you have solved all questions for the time being.
Franz Kafka

Cucumber, Walnut, and Orange

A wonderfully refreshing recipe for a hot summer's day. The walnuts add a satisfying crunch, a bit of protein, and are a good source of vitamin E. This recipe is ideal as a snack, or as part of dietary regime. Garnish with fresh dill if desired.

Ingredients
Cucumber
Orange
Walnut
Salt
Black pepper
Sesame Oil

Preparation
Slice the cucumber thinly. Segment the orange by cutting off the top and bottom of the fruit, then carefully slicing down with a sharp knife, removing both the outer and inner skin so that the fruit's flesh is revealed. Cut both sides of the segment and scoop out the flesh. Remove pips and any remaining white pith. Break the walnuts into small chunks and mix everything together. Add seasoning to taste.

Dressing
Sesame oil, salt, pepper and just a tiny amount of vinegar if desired.

Get people back into the kitchen and combat the trend toward processed food and fast food.
Andrew Weil

Potato, Spring Onion, and Ham

A nourishing salad to fill an empty stomach. Red potatoes are good for salads, but any will do. A nice accompaniment to most dishes.

Ingredients

Potato
Spring Onion
Ham
Red Pepper
Salt
Olive Oil
White Wine Vinegar

Preparation

Peel the potato, half and quarter with a knife. Boil until medium soft. Allow to cool, and dice into small squares. Dice the spring onion and cut the ham into long strips. Place ingredients into a mixing bowl and toss lightly. Be liberal with the olive oil as it is readily absorbed into the potato. Sprinkle on ground red pepper.

Dressing

Olive oil, white wine vinegar, salt, and a little mustard if desired.

I saw few die of hunger; of eating, a hundred thousand.
Benjamin Franklin

Zucchini, Radish, and Date

This is a wholesome dish and provides plenty of tangy taste and nourishment either as a salad on its own, or as an accompaniment. The crumbly cheese and sweetness of the date work nicely together, and are complemented by the 'hot' and bitter of the radish and zucchini.

Ingredients

Zucchini (courgette)
Radish
Date
Crumbly Cheese
Lemon Zest
Olive Oil
Lemon Juice
Salt
Pepper

Preparation

Thinly slice the zucchini (courgette) and radish, dice the date and grate the lemon zest. Place all ingredients into a mixing bowl and stir with a fork to ensure everything is well coated with the dressing.

Dressing

Extra virgin olive oil and lemon juice are all that is needed to draw out the flavors in this dish.

One should eat to live, not live to eat.
Moliere

Cannellini Bean and Pear

This unusual combination is both nutritious and full of interesting flavor. The parsley gives an earthiness that emerges with every bite.

Ingredients

Cannellini bean
Pear
Parsley
Olive Oil
Lemon juice, or fruit vinegar
Salt
Pepper

Preparation

Follow the packet instructions for cooking the beans. If using canned beans, be sure to rinse and dry thoroughly. Dice the pear and chop the parsley finely. Mix all the ingredients into a mixing bowl and serve chilled.

Dressing

Olive oil, lemon juice, or fruit vinegar being careful not to overwhelm the subtle sweetness of the pear.

Statistics show that of those who contract the habit of eating, very few survive.
George Bernard Shaw

Fig, Radicchio, and Endive

This recipe provides a wholesome meal or starter. The bitter taste of the radicchio and endive (chicory) are offset by the sweetness of the figs. Crumbly blue cheese complements the fig and adds a smooth, rich texture.

Ingredients

Fig
Radicchio
Endive
Crumbly Blue Cheese
Olive Oil
Balsamic Vinegar
Salt
Pepper

Preparation

Chop the radicchio and endive, quarter the fig and add the cheese. Mix together with the dressing.

Dressing

Olive oil, balsamic vinegar to taste (being careful not to smother the flavors and sweetness). Add salt and pepper.

> Too many people just eat to consume calories. Try dining for a change.
> *John Walters*

Chinese Cabbage, Bamboo Shoots

A salad with an Asian twist, and a perfect accompaniment to tofu, egg, and fish.

Preparation

Chop the cabbage and spring onions then add bamboo shoots. Toss with the sesame oil dressing and top with sesame seeds and ground red pepper.

Ingredients

Chinese cabbage
Bamboo shoot
Spring onion
Sesame seed
Sesame oil
Lemon juice
Red pepper (ground)
Sea salt

Dressing

Mix together the sesame oil, lemon juice and salt.

> Gluttony is an emotional escape,
> a sign something is eating us.
> *Peter De Vries*

Carrot, Radish, and Nuts

There is a lot of goodness packed into this meal, so it is ideal as a small lunch or dinner, especially if you are on a diet.

Preparation

Finely grate the carrot and radish and place into a mixing bowl. Chop the nuts into small pieces and add to the carrot and radish. Finely chop the parsley and onion, crush the garlic and place everything into a mixing bowl. Mix all the ingredients adding seasoning and dressing.

Ingredients

Carrot
Radish
Onion
Garlic
Walnut
Cashew nut
Parsley
White wine vinegar
Olive oil
Salt
Black Pepper

Dressing

Oil oil, white wine vinegar, and seasoning.

The food that enters the mind must be watched as closely as the food that enters the body.
Pat Buchanan

Tomato, Feta Cheese, and Olive

This is a classic Mediterranean-style salad, and is featured in many recipe books. The skill, however, is in choosing the best ingredients. The tomatoes need to be full of flavor and the feta cheese needs to be of good quality.

Preparation

Slice, or dice the tomato, cube the feta cheese, and thinly slice the onion. Layer the ingredients on top of each other starting with the tomato. Pour the olive oil over the top followed by the balsamic vinegar, or the lemon juice.

Ingredients

Tomato
Onion
Black olive
Feta cheese
Oregano
Salt
Black pepper

Dressing

Extra virgin olive oil, balsamic vinegar. Try adding them separately as opposed to mixing them together into a dressing.

Never order food in excess of your body weight.
Erma Bombeck

Green Salad

Packed with goodness and vitamins, this all green salad is a wonderful accompaniment to fish. Use butterhead lettuce for its soft and creamy texture. Either sunflower sprouts, or alfalfa, or mustard and cress work well.

Ingredients

Lettuce (butterhead)
Cucumber
Spring onion
Green beans
Parsley
Sunflower sprouts (or mustard and cress)
Olive oil
Balsamic vinegar
Salt
Pepper

Preparation

Boil the green beans until they soften slightly, drain thoroughly, and allow to cool. Chop the lettuce, spring onions, and finely chop the parsley. Add all ingredients into a mixing bowl and toss together with the oil and vinegar. Season to taste and serve chilled.

Dressing

Olive oil, balsamic vinegar, salt and black pepper.

"To keep the body in good health is a duty... otherwise we shall not be able to keep our mind strong and clear.
Buddha

Tomato with Corn Puree

Surprise your guests with this delightful stuffed tomato appetiser, or starter. Full round, ripe tomatoes are best.

Ingredients

Corn
Cream cheese
Tomatoes
Parsley
Lemon juice and zest
Salt
Black pepper

Preparation

Add the corn, cream cheese, lemon juice, parsley, and seasoning into a blender and mix until they become a smooth mixture. Slice the tomatoes in half and scoop out the inner flesh. Spoon in the puree, top with the lemon zest and drizzle over the top with olive oil.

Dressing

No extra dressing is needed since lemon juice and olive oil are already present.

Good health is not something we can buy. However, it can be an extremely valuable savings account.
Anne Wilson Schaef

Curried Egg Mayonnaise

A delicious, wholesome meal consisting of curried eggs on a bed of raw spinach with garlic whole-wheat croutons. A wonderful starter or light lunch.

Preparation

Boils the eggs for about ten minutes, let cool and peel off the shell. Slice into halves and scoop out the solid yoke into a mixing bowl. Add a thick mayonnaise, a good pinch of curry powder and salt. Mix with a fork until the consistency is smooth. Place back into the egg white halves. Heat some olive oil in a pan and lightly fry the crushed garlic, then add the bread cubes. Fry until evenly browned.

Ingredients

Boiled eggs
Baby leaf spinach
Whole-wheat bread
Garlic
Mayonnaise
Curry powder
Salt

Dressing

No extra dressing is needed since mayonnaise is already present in the recipe.

He who has health, has hope; and he who has hope, has everything.
Thomas Carlyle

Tomato and Cucumber Gelatin

Although not strictly a salad, this dish uses vegetables is a delightful and refreshing way.

Preparation

Place the tomatoes in a saucepan of hot water for a minute or two. Remove from the saucepan, peel off the skin, and liquidize. Season and add a drop of Tabasco and Worcestershire (pronounced *wooster*) sauce. Peel a cucumber and liquidize. Force the liquids through a sieve (separately) to remove seeds and lumps. Following the instructions on the gelatin packet, prepare the cucumber gelatin first and pour into a small dish. Make sure the dish is brushed with olive oil or water. Once it has set, prepare the tomato gelatin and pour over the cucumber gelatin. Refrigerate until set.

Ingredients

Tomato
Cucumber
Gelatin
Salt
Black pepper
Tabasco
Worcestershire sauce

Garnish

Black olives, sour cream, and parsley.

"A healthy attitude is contagious but don't wait to catch it from others. Be a carrier.
Tom Stoppard

Carrot, Pine Nut, and Parsley

Lots of satisfying crunch and goodness in this light, simple salad. Make sure you use large, fresh, organic carrots that are usually packed with sweetness.

Preparation

Coarsely grate the carrot and place into a mixing bowl with pine nuts, sesame seeds and finely chopped parsley. Add sesame oil, lemon juice, seasoning and mix together.

Ingredients

Organic carrots
Pine nuts
Sesame seeds
Sesame oil
Parsley
Salt
Black pepper
Lemon juice

Dressing

Add the sesame oil and lemon juice directly into the salad.

Salad can get a bad rap. People think of bland and watery iceberg lettuce, but in fact, salads are an art form, from the simplest rendition to a colorful kitchen-sink approach.
Marcus Samuelsson

Tofu, Shallots, and Raisons

Tofu is a good source of alternative protein but its blandness takes getting used to. The sweetness from the raisons, and the sharpness from the shallots complement the tofu. Adding a little turmeric rounds off the flavors nicely.

Preparation

Tofu is usually washed and either steamed or microwaved for a minute before consuming. Chop into little squares, slice the shallots and place into a mixing bowl with the raisons, turmeric and sesame oil. Add some green such as lightly boiled broccoli, or coriander. Mix together with the dressing.

Ingredients

Tofu
Shallots
Raisons
Broccoli (or coriander)
Sesame oil
Lemon juice
Turmeric
Salt
Pepper

Dressing

Sesame oil and lemon juice.

Sprinkle a little thought over any dish, and watch as creative spendour unfolds.
Pierre Charmant

Rice, Coriander, and Strawberries

If a salad can taste as good as it looks, this one passes muster. I've used a black rice, but brown works equally well. Several contrasting tastes and textures make this an interesting dinner party side dish or accompaniment.

Ingredients

Black or brown rice
Strawberries
Coriander
Red onion
Sesame Oil
Wine or fruit vinegar
Salt
Pepper

Preparation

Cook the rice and allow to cool. Cut medium sized strawberries into quarters, slice the onion thinly, and remove most of the stalk from the coriander. Place in a mixing bowl with seasoning and the dressing. If you don't like raw onion, sweat (fry with a lid) them in a pan to soften them.

Dressing

Sesame oil and either a small amount wine or fruit vinegar being careful not to smother the taste of the strawberries.

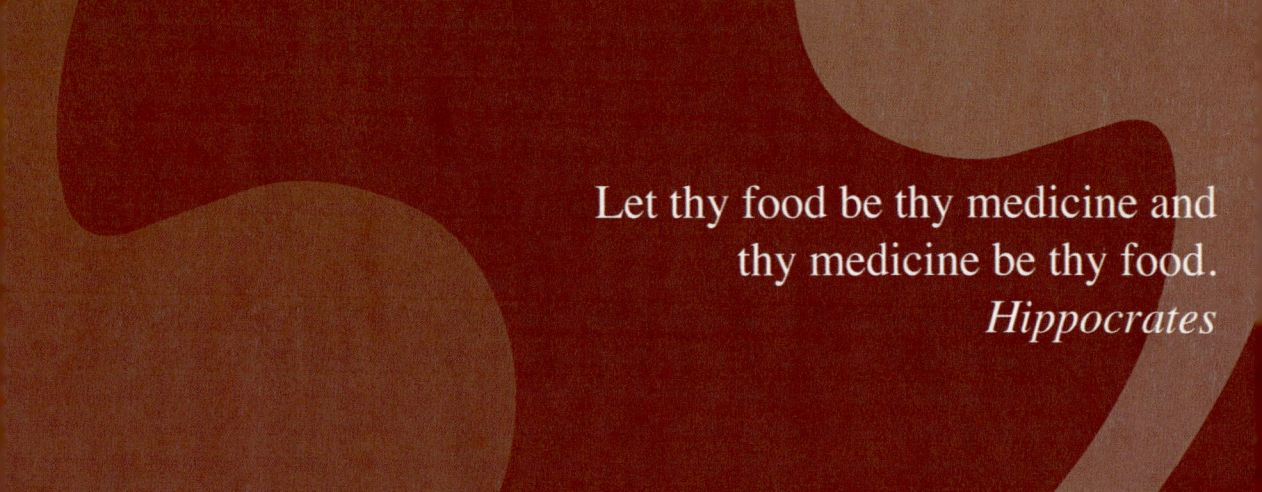

Let thy food be thy medicine and thy medicine be thy food.
Hippocrates

Beetroot, Yoghurt, and Chives

A salad version of the Russian soup Borscht, comprising raw beetroot and yoghurt. Adding apple or pear adds a bit more sweetness and interest making this a healthy starter.

Ingredients

Beetroot (raw, or lightly cooked)
Onion
Chives
Yoghurt
Apple (optional)

Preparation

Finely grate the beetroot and allow excess juices to drain. Finely chop some onion and mix with the beets. Add a tea spoon of yoghurt, and seasoning to taste. Garnish with chives and yoghurt.

Dressing

The yoghurt is the dressing.

Our bodies are our gardens – our wills are our gardeners.
William Shakespeare

Fennel, Goat Cheese, and Grapes

This is a delightful combination of the sweetness of grapes and the savory flavor of goat cheese. Fennel has a wonderfully subtle flavor that adds interest and crunch. Wrapped in a radicchio leaf, the salad is a good side dish or starter ideal for entertaining.

Ingredients

Fennel
Goat cheese
White seedless grapes
Radicchio
Olive oil
White wine vinegar
Salt
Pepper

Preparation

Dice the fennel into small chunks, dice the goat cheese into small squares, halve the grapes and place into a mixing bowl with the olive oil, vinegar and seasoning. Mix together well.

Dressing

Use a generous portion of olive oil and a small amount of white wine vinegar. Add salt and ground black pepper.

To keep the body in good health is a duty, for otherwise we shall not be able to trim the lamp of wisdom, and keep our mind strong and clear. Water surrounds the lotus flower, but does not wet its petals.
Buddha

Celery, Radish, and Dried Apricots

Plenty of crunch with a touch of sweetness to offset the hot taste of the radish. A great accompaniment, snack, or combination with other salads. Easy and quick to prepare.

Ingredients

Celery
Radish
Dried apricots
Olive oil
Wine vinegar
Salt
Pepper

Preparation

Chop the celery into small chunks and slice the radish thinly. Dice the dried apricot into small cubes and place all ingredients into a mixing bowl. Add the dressing and mix well. Serve chilled.

Dressing

Use a thick extra virgin olive oil together with a drop of vinegar. Avoid balsamic or malt vinegars. Pour separately into the mixing bowl with seasoning and toss well.

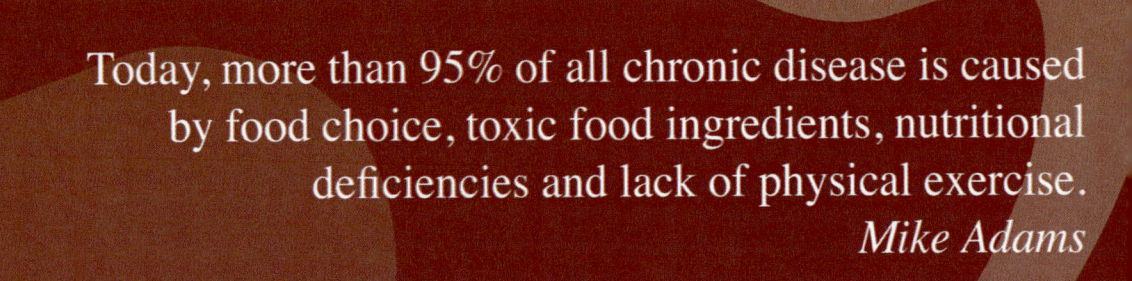

Today, more than 95% of all chronic disease is caused by food choice, toxic food ingredients, nutritional deficiencies and lack of physical exercise.
Mike Adams

Red Cabbage, Peppers, and Tomato

Lots of vitamins packed into this red salad. There is plenty going on here taste-wise so it makes a nice stand-alone salad, or accompaniment to fish.

Ingredients

Red cabbage
Red pepper
Tomato
Beetroot
Parsley
Salt
Pepper
Olive Oil
Vinegar

Preparation

Dice the pepper and tomato, finely slice the red cabbage and beetroot, chop the parsley and place in a mixing bowl with seasoning and dressing. Mix thoroughly.

Dressing

Olive oil works well with either a wine or balsamic vinegar.

Healing in a matter of time, but it is sometimes also a matter of opportunity.
Hippocrates

Lentils, Zucchini, Spinach

Lentils have been eaten by man throughout the ages, and have a comparatively high level of protein. Mango chunks liven up this salad making it ideal for a side dish, or accompaniment.

Ingredients

Spinach
Zucchini
Lentils
Mango
Salt
Pepper
Mixed herbs (dried)
Olive Oil
White wine vinegar

Preparation

Slice the zucchini and marinate for several hours in one part vinegar to one part water, mixed herbs, salt and pepper. Drain thoroughly. Cook the lentils according to instructions on the packet and let cool. Dice the mango, drain the zucchini and mix all ingredients in a mixing boil.

Dressing

Olive oil or a nut oil if preferred, but not too much vinegar (if any) since the zucchini will already be marinated. Add salt and pepper to taste.

The part can never be well unless the whole is well.
Plato

Banana, Nuts, and Fig

This is a sweet salad for those who need a little pep in their step. The fiber from bananas, the health benefits of omega 3 from the nuts, and the digestive benefits of figs makes this a nourishing meal.

Ingredients

Banana
Figs
Mixed nuts (cashew, walnut, almonds, hazelnuts)
Parsley
Pepper
Olive oil
Balsamic Vinegar (optional)

Preparation

Slice the banana, halve or quarter the figs being careful to remove the hard stem, finely chop the nuts and parsley. Mix all the ingredients in a bowl.

Dressing

This recipe works without a dressing, but a little olive oil helps blend the flavors. A small amount of balsamic can be added if desired.

> It is my view that a vegetarian manner of living by its purely physical effect on the human temperament would most beneficially influence the lot of mankind.
> *Albert Einstein*

Carrot, Zucchini, and Chives

A light, refreshing salad using yellow zucchini. A nice accompaniment to chicken or fish dishes. Uncooked zucchini has a soft texture and can be eaten raw.

Ingredients

Carrot
Zucchini (courgette)
Chives
Sesame oil
Sesame seeds
Lemon juice
Salt
Black pepper

Preparation

Cut the carrot and zucchini into 2-3 inch lengths. Halve them down their length and use a potato peeler to create thin slices. Chop the chives into shorter lengths and add all ingredients into a mixing bowl. Mix thoroughly and serve chilled.

Dressing

Sesame oil, sesame seeds, lemon juice, salt and pepper.

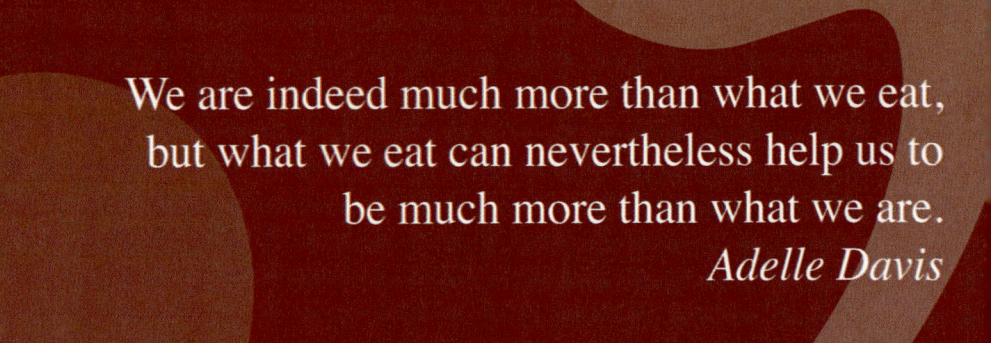

> We are indeed much more than what we eat, but what we eat can nevertheless help us to be much more than what we are.
> *Adelle Davis*

Brussels Sprouts and Mushrooms

Since this recipe requires minimal cooking, it's perhaps more a vegetarian dish than a salad. Brussels, however, are such a good source of cancer inhibiting properties no health-minded recipe book is complete without them.

Ingredients

Brussels sprouts
Button mushrooms
Oregano
Soy sauce
Butter
White wine vinegar
Pepper

Preparation

Steam the brussels to retain the goodness, and bake (cover with foil) the sliced mushrooms in the butter, soy sauce and black pepper. Mix all ingredients together and serve warm.

Dressing

Add a little salt, or a dash of lemon juice if desired.

Healthy citizens are the greatest asset any country can have.
Winston S. Churchill

Pinto, Green Bean, and Beetroot

A hearty and wholesome salad. Pinto beans are a good source of protein and fiber. Beans must be cooked.

Ingredients

Pinto beans
Green beans
Beetroot
Olive oil
Balsamic vinegar
Salt
Pepper

Preparation

Thoroughly cook the pinto beans according to the instructions on the packet. Lightly boil or steam the green beans until tender but not too soft. Slice and boil the beetroot until soft. Drain the green beans and beetroot and allow to cool. Place all the ingredients into a bowl and mix thoroughly. Serve at room temperature.

Dressing

Olive oil, balsamic vinegar, salt and pepper.

If we are creating ourselves all the time, then it is never too late to begin creating the bodies we want instead of the ones we mistakenly assume we are stuck with.
Deepak Chopra

Spinach, Fennel, and Walnuts

Fennel is somewhere between a herb and vegetable. It is in fact related to the carrot. The bulb can be eaten raw and is a useful ingredient in salads. The dill-like leaves are mild and can be added as a garnish. This is a light salad but is wholesome and subtly flavorsome.

Ingredients
Baby spinach
Fennel
Walnuts
Sesame oil
Lemon juice
Salt
Pepper

Preparation
You may wish to remove an outer layer of the fennel bulb if it is tough. Dice into small pieces and add to the spinach leaves. Pull off a few of the fennel leaves to use as a garnish. Break the walnuts into small pieces using a tenderiser. Place all ingredients into a bowl and mix.

Dressing
Sesame oil, white wine vinegar, salt, black pepper.

> Nothing would be more tiresome than eating and drinking if God had not made them a pleasure as well as a necessity.
> *Voltaire*

Corn, Tomato, and Leek

This combination works so well and provides a nourishing meal or side dish. Substitute red bell pepper for tomato, and onion for leek. Add goat cheese for a really nutritious meal.

Ingredients

Corn
Tomato (or red bell pepper)
Leek (or onion)
Olive oil
White wine vinegar
Salt
Black pepper

Preparation

Boil or steam the corn and remove the corn from its husk. Wash thoroughly if using canned corn. Leeks can be eaten raw, but ensure they are washed as dirt often collects inside the leaves. The lighter the color the more tender, so the dark part of the leek can be discarded. Dice the tomato and slice the leek into thin rings. Mix all ingredients in a bowl and serve chilled.

Dressing

Olive oil, white wine vinegar, salt black pepper.

> To eat is a necessity, but to eat intelligently is an art.
> *La Rochefoucauld*

Brown Rice, Carrot, and Cress

Wild or brown rice is given preference over white rice, and mustard and cress is a better choice than alfalfa or similar, in my opinion. A delicious, filling salad to accompany cold meats or fish.

Ingredients

Brown (or wild) rice
Carrot
Mustard and cress (or similar)
Olive oil
White wine vinegar (or Japanese rice vinegar)
Salt
Cayenne pepper (or black pepper)

Preparation

Cook the rice, drain and allow to cool. Coarsely grate the carrot and place in a bowl with all the other ingredients. Mix and serve chilled.

Dressing

Olive oil, white wine vinegar (or rice vinegar), salt, cayenne pepper (or black pepper).

Those who think they have no time for healthy eating,
will sooner or later have to find time for illness.
Edward Stanley

Warm, Winter Salad

I've named this salad a 'winter' salad because fried onions take the chill off the other vegetables, making it palatable to eat even in the colder months of the year. It is the most quintessential of all salads, employing lettuce, tomato, and cucumber. Butterhead lettuce adds a wonderfully silky texture and works best with this recipe.

Ingredients

Butterhead Lettuce
Tomato
Cucumber
Oregano
Onion
Butter (or olive oil)
Lemon juice (or vinegar)
Garlic
Salt
Black Pepper

Preparation

Wash the lettuce and dry very thoroughly. Slice the tomato and cucumber and place in a bowl with the dry lettuce. Slice the onion and fry in the butter. Add seasoning, oregano and garlic, placing a lid over the saucepan to sweat the onion until soft. Toss the hot onions into the salad, mixing thoroughly with lemon juice or vinegar. Serve immediately.

Dressing

The dressing comes from the butter-coated onions. Add the lemon juice in the final mix together with any seasoning to taste.

Knowledge is knowing that a tomato is a fruit.
Wisdom is knowing not to put it in a fruit salad.
Brian O'Driscoll

Tomato, Tofu, and Spring Onion

A delightful and refreshing salad that works with everything. Tofu is a good source of protein so this is an ideal salad for those wishing to lose weight.

Ingredients

Tomato
Spring onion
Tofu (medium firm)
Parsley
Lettuce leaf (optional)
Olive oil
Balsamic vinegar
Salt
Black pepper

Preparation

Wash the tofu and cut into small cubes. Cube the tomato, and slice the spring onion into small pieces. Chop the parsley finely and place all ingredients into a mixing bowl. Mix thoroughly and compress gently into a small container. Turn the container upside down onto a lettuce leaf and serve chilled.

Dressing

Olive oil, balsamic vinegar, salt, black pepper.

As I see it, a green salad is an open invitation to carrots, onions, mushrooms, tomatoes, and the sprouts that grow in jars on my kitchen counter.
Victoria Moran

Celery, Grapes, and Nuts

The celery and grapes work well together, making this a succulent salad. Pine nuts (or walnuts if preferred), adds nourishment. A good between-course, palate cleaner and accompaniment to fish, or chicken.

Ingredients

Red grapes
Celery
Pine nuts (or walnuts)
Olive oil
White wine vinegar
Salt
White Pepper

Preparation

Cut the grapes into halves (remove pips) and slice the celery into small pieces. Place all ingredients into a mixing bowl and mix well. Use vinegar sparingly to avoid over-powering the grapes.

Dressing

Olive oil, white wine vinegar, salt, white pepper.

Why not give your digestive system
the break it probably deserves.
James Clarke

Cauliflower, Radish, and Zucchini

Cauliflowers are a rather neglected vegetable, especially when it comes to salads. It can, however, be eaten raw and is highly nutritious.

Ingredients

Cauliflower
Radish
Zucchini (courgette)
Raisons
Olive oil (or sesame oil)
White wine vinegar
Salt
Black pepper

Preparation

Grate the cauliflower, radish and zucchini finely. Add in the rest of the ingredients and mix. Gently compress into a small rounded cup or container and lower contents onto a plate.

Dressing

Olive oil (or sesame oil), white wine vinegar, salt, black pepper.

A man can live and be healthy without killing animals for food; therefore, if he eats meat, he participates in taking animal life merely for the sake of his appetite.
Leo Tolstoy

Beans, Onion, and Cheese

For those who want a break from all those vegetables, this is a pleaser. Kidney beans must be well cooked.

Ingredients

Kidney beans
Cheddar Cheese
Black olives
Onion
Parsley
Olive oil
Balsamic vinegar
Salt
Black pepper

Preparation

Cook beans thoroughly according to packet instructions. Use canned if you haven't time to cook them, but wash and drain thoroughly. Grate the cheese, slice the onion and chop the parsley finely. Place all ingredients into a bowl and mix well.

Dressing

Olive oil, balsamic vinegar, salt, black pepper.

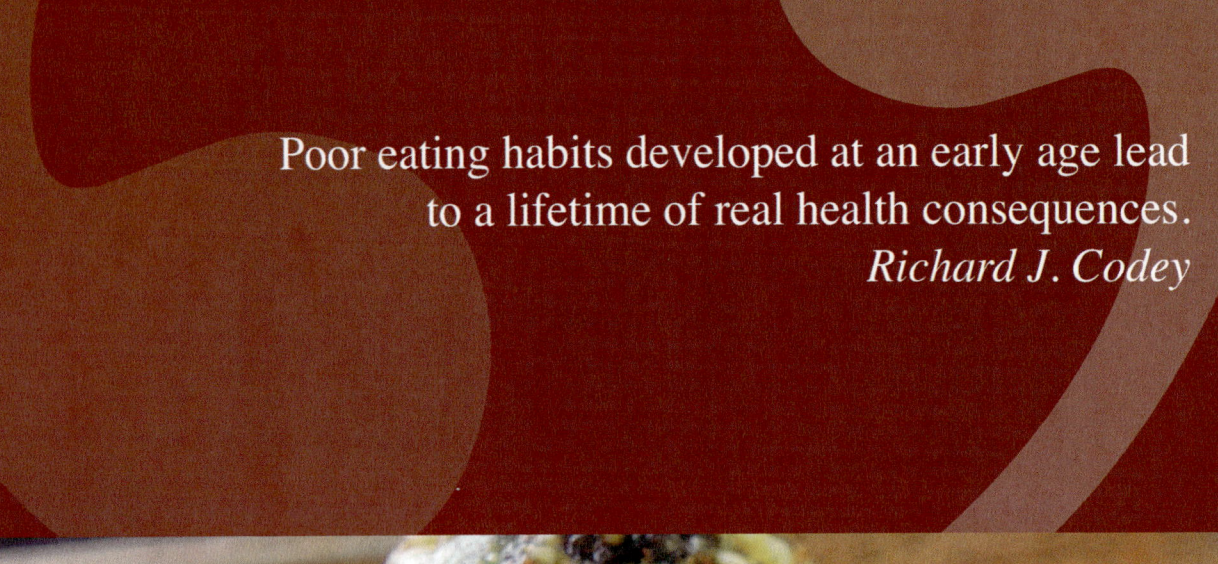

> Poor eating habits developed at an early age lead to a lifetime of real health consequences.
> *Richard J. Codey*

Nut and Raisin Balls

This makes a good accompaniment to other salad dishes. It also makes an ideal between-meal snack.

Ingredients

Mixed nuts
Raisins
Lemon zest
Cilantro (coriander)
Sesame oil
Rice vinegar
Salt
White pepper

Preparation

Place all ingredients into a blender until finely chopped. Mold into small balls using your hands, and serve with carrot and lettuce garnish.

Dressing

Sesame oil, rice vinegar (use sparingly), salt, white pepper.

If you can eat 70 percent raw or introduce raw into your diet, it will help your health.
Carol Alt

Root Vegetables

This recipe uses sweet potato, parsnip and turnip as the base for the salad, but rutabaga (swede), or carrots can also be used. The vegetables are lightly steamed to soften them. It makes a wonderful accompaniment served warm.

Ingredients

Sweet potato (or rutabaga),
Parsnip (or carrot)
Turnip
Thyme
Olive oil
Lemon zest
Salt
Red pepper

Preparation

Dice vegetables into small cubes, then steam or boil separately as they need different cooking times to soften. Sweet potato softens quite quickly so be careful not over cook. Let cool and mix in the rest of the ingredients.

Dressing

Oil oil, lemon juice, red pepper, and salt.

Any food that requires enhancing by the use of chemical substances should in no way be considered a food.
John H. Tobe

Sprouts, Kiwi, and Avocado

This is a delightfully refreshing and nutritious salad. I've used mixed wild Hawaiian herbs, but mustard and cress or similar will work just as well.

Ingredients

Mustard and cress (or similar)
Avocado
Kiwi
Almond flakes
Olive Oil
Lemon juice
Salt
Black pepper

Preparation

Slice the avocado and kiwi, and mix in with the rest of the ingredients. Serve chilled

Dressing

Oil oil, lemon juice, salt, black pepper.

[We] subsidize high-fructose corn syrup
in this country, but not carrots...
Michael Pollan

Carrots, Chilly, Olives, and Nuts

If you can find yellow carrots or a bag of assorted colors, this recipe makes a head-turner for entertaining. The olives add flavor and the chili pepper adds some spice. The hot sensation from chillies is caused by chemicals that fool the brain into thinking something hot has been placed in the mouth.

Ingredients

Yellow Carrots (or mixed colors)
Black olives
Mixed nuts
Chili peppers
Sesame oil
Rice vinegar
Salt

Preparation

Coarsely grate the carrot, remove stones from the olives and slice into halves, dice the chili peppers into small pieces, and grind the nuts using either a tenderiser, or food processor. Place all ingredients into a mixing bowl. Mix well and serve chilled.

Dressing

Sesame oil, rice vinegar, and salt.

"While the surgeon general is raising alarms over the epidemic of obesity, the president is signing farm bills designed to keep the river of cheap corn flowing...
Michael Pollan

Endive, Grapefruit, and Dates

A mouth watering and refreshing salad that will set off the taste buds. The bitterness of the endive and sharpness of the grapefruit are tempered with the sweetness of the dates and the coolness of the mint. A nice stand alone salad for a hot summers day.

Ingredients

Endive (chicory)
Grapefruit
Dates
Mint
Sesame oil
Salt
Black pepper
Rice vinegar

Preparation

Segment the grapefruit by first cutting off the peel from the top and bottom of the fruit. Then cut off the remaining peel ensuring enough is removed to reveal the flesh. Cut the flesh away from the segments, so the fruit is completely free of all skin, pith, and pips. Chop the endive and dates into medium sized pieces, and finely chop the mint. Add all ingredients into a bowl, mix well, and serve chilled. Vinegar is optional as the grapefruit has ample tartness.

Dressing

Sesame oil, salt, black pepper, rice vinegar (if desired).

Made in the USA
Las Vegas, NV
10 December 2024